Genre Exposito...

Essential Question
How can learning about animals help you respect them?

African Cats

by Vanessa York

Introduction 2

Chapter 1
Cats, Cats, Cats. 4

Chapter 2
Little Big Cats 10

Conclusion. 13

Respond to Reading 15

PAIRED READ How Leopard Got His Spots 16

Glossary/Index 19

STEM Focus on Science 20

Introduction

You can find members of the cat family all over the world. Whatever their size or **species**, cats are remarkable.

Cats have special adaptations, or features, that make them amazing **predators**. They nearly all have **retractable** claws and sharp eyesight. They have muscles that are suited to short bursts of speed. They are also powerful jumpers and climbers.

All species of cats are excellent hunters.

Perhaps the most fascinating cats are found in Africa. It is home to lions, leopards, and cheetahs, as well as servals, caracals, and golden cats.

A ranger watches a lion family sleeping in the shade.

African Cat Territory

Africa

Where lions, leopards, cheetahs, servals, caracals, and golden cats live

3

Chapter 1

Cats, Cats, Cats

Lions and leopards are big African cats. Big cats look and behave a lot like most other cats. However, only big cats can roar.

Lions

A lion's roar is so loud that it can be heard almost five miles away. Unlike most cats, which are **solitary**, lions live in family groups. These family groups are called prides. A pride may have up to three males and a dozen females, called lionesses. Young males leave the family group. They may take over another pride by fighting and overcoming another male. Some may live in small groups with other males.

All the lionesses in a pride are related.

Hunting zebras takes a lot of work.

Lions usually live on the **savannah**. A pride's **territory** may be as large as 100 square miles. It is the males' job to defend this territory. The females' job is to provide food for the pride. Lionesses work together to hunt zebras and other **prey**. Lions only catch one in five of the animals they stalk. If they get the chance, lions steal kills from hyenas and other cats.

The Lion's Mane

Scientists used to think that the male lion's mane was to help protect its neck when fighting. However, lions attack the back and hindquarters, not the neck. Now scientists have discovered that a full mane attracts females.

Leopards

Leopards are the smallest of the big cats. They like to live in forests and near rivers. They can adapt to other places, such as mountains and savannah. They are generally solitary and mostly **nocturnal**. They like to hunt at night and rest during the day. Their spots allow them to blend in with their surroundings, whether it is leaves or long grass. This makes them very successful at catching birds, reptiles, or mammals unaware.

Leopards are great climbers. They like to sleep in the branches of trees.

Brand X Pictures/PunchStock

Conservation Status of
Leopards

Extinct

Threatened

► **Near threatened** ◄

Least concern

Leopards never stay in one place for long. The only exception to this is when a female has cubs. She hides them for a couple of months. Then they are able to follow her and start learning to hunt.

A leopard's spots are called rosettes.

Leopard Body Language

You can tell a leopard by its spots, and you can often tell what it's thinking by looking at its tail! Body language is one important way that cats communicate.

normal stance

stalking

frustration

submission

dominant walk

Cheetahs

Cheetahs are known for their speed. They can go from 0 to 60 miles per hour in just three seconds. This makes them the fastest land mammals, and faster than a lot of cars. They have small heads and long legs, making them powerful. Their claws are only partly retractable. This gives them good traction when they run.

Unlike lions and leopards, cheetahs do not roar. They purr, chirp, and growl.

Cheetahs drink every two or three days.

Conservation Status of Cheetahs

Extinct

Threatened

► Near threatened ◄

Least concern

Cheetahs stalk prey, such as gazelles and warthogs, on the savannah. When the prey is about 60 feet away, they sprint to catch it. They use their tail like a rudder to change direction quickly. The cheetah can only keep up its speed for a short time. If it doesn't catch its prey quickly, the cheetah gives up.

A cheetah's power is speed, not strength.

Adapted for Speed

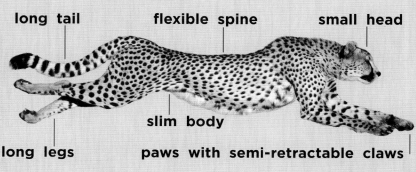

long tail   flexible spine   small head

slim body

long legs   paws with semi-retractable claws

Chapter 2
Little Big Cats

Little big cats are much smaller than lions and leopards. They are still a lot bigger and heavier than the cats we keep at home!

Servals

Servals are medium-sized spotted cats. They have small heads with enormous ears. They have excellent hearing and can even hear the rodents they hunt moving underground. They also hunt hares, birds, reptiles, insects, and fish.

Servals have the longest legs of any cat in relation to their size.

When servals pounce, they can leap up to 12 feet from a standstill. They also use this ability to leap into the air and catch birds in flight.

Serval kittens are raised by their mother alone. She meets all their requirements until they are about one year old. Servals prefer to live on the savannah. They can also inhabit rocky areas or forests. Like the cheetah, the serval purrs, growls, and chirps.

The serval leaps, landing on its target with great force.

Conservation Status of
Servals

Extinct

Threatened

Near threatened

► **Least concern** ◄

Charles Nolder/Alamy

African Golden Cats

One of the most mysterious cats is the African golden cat. These shy cats like to live in thick forests. Scientists find it hard to study them in the wild.

African golden cats are not often seen in the wild.

Caracals

Caracals are medium-sized cats with tufted ears. Caracals prefer to live in a semidesert **habitat**. They also live on the savannah and in forests. Caracals are respected for their incredible skill at hunting birds.

Caracals' excellent hearing helps them hunt.

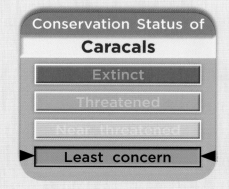

Conservation Status of
Caracals

Extinct

Threatened

Near threatened

Least concern

Conclusion

Like wildlife populations everywhere, African cats are threatened. Big cats, such as lions and leopards, may soon be endangered. The biggest threat is the loss of their habitat. Human activities, such as building roads and farming, are leaving less space for wildlife.

Illegal hunting is also a problem in some places. There are protected wildlife areas in parts of Africa. Outside those areas, lions, leopards, servals, and cheetahs have been killed for their beautiful fur. They have also been killed for use in traditional medicines.

These are difficult problems to fix. Teaching people about the problem can help. People can choose not to buy products made from these animals.

African cats may also be killed by farmers to protect their livestock. Conservation organizations are working with farmers. They may remove big cats and relocate them in a safe reserve, away from farmers.

Many people are working to protect African cat habitats. They are also working to promote conservation. We need to make sure these fascinating animals survive.

A ranger checks a young cheetah's heartbeat.

Summarize

Use details from the text to summarize *African Cats*. Your diagram may help you.

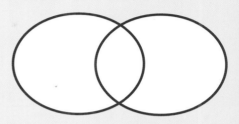

Text Evidence

1. How do you know *African Cats* is expository text? Identify the text features. GENRE

2. What are two differences between lions and leopards? COMPARE AND CONTRAST

3. What is the meaning of the word *overcoming* on page 4? Use paragraph clues to help you figure out the meaning. CONTEXT CLUES

4. Write a paragraph that compares servals with leopards. How are they alike? How are they different? WRITE ABOUT READING

Compare Texts

Read how Leopard became an even better hunter than he was already.

How Leopard Got His Spots

Long ago, Leopard was plain yellow, like the savannah where he lived. When he went hunting, he was almost invisible.

Giraffe and Zebra were Leopard's favorite prey. They didn't know which way to jump to avoid Leopard's devastating pounce.

Illustration: Natalia Vasquez

They thought long and hard about what to do. After much discussion, they decided to move to the forest.

Zebra trotted off into the shadows of the trees. Giraffe followed at a more leisurely pace. They were safe.

They were not to feel safe for long. Leopard followed them to the forest. His yellowness made him stand out like a sunflower in the shadows. Zebra and Giraffe saw him coming every time, and they ran away. Leopard grew very hungry indeed.

At last, Leopard asked a man to help him. Leopard explained his problem, and the man had an idea. He dipped his fingers into black ink and painted spots all over Leopard's yellow fur.

Now Leopard blended into the forest shadows and the savannah, too. He was a better hunter than ever. He was soon feeling very well fed.

Make Connections

What do you admire or respect about the cats that you read about? ESSENTIAL QUESTION

From what you read in *African Cats*, which parts of *How Leopard Got His Spots* are facts? TEXT TO TEXT

Glossary

habitat *(HA-buh-tat)* the area where an animal naturally lives *(page 12)*

nocturnal *(nok-TURN-uhl)* happening or appearing at night *(page 6)*

predators *(PRE-duh-turz)* animals that eats other animals *(page 2)*

prey *(PRAY)* an animal that is hunted by another animal for food *(page 5)*

retractable *(ree-TRAK-tuh-buhl)* able to be extended and pulled back, like a cat's claws *(page 2)*

savannah *(suh-VAN-uh)* a flat, grassy plains *(page 5)*

solitary *(SOL-uh-te-ree)* existing alone *(page 4)*

species *(SPEE-sheez)* a group of living things that have many characteristics in common *(page 2)*

territory *(TER-i-tor-ee)* a large area of land; region *(page 5)*

Index

African golden cats, *3, 12*

caracals, *3, 12*

cheetahs, *3, 8, 9, 11, 13, 14*

habitats, *12–14*

leopards, *3, 4, 6–8, 10, 13*

lions, *3–5, 8, 10, 13*

prey, *5, 9, 10*

servals, *3, 10, 11, 13*

Focus on Science

Purpose To understand that living things need the right requirements to thrive

What to Do

Step 1 ➤ Fill three small containers with soil.

Step 2 ➤ Plant seeds, such as pumpkin, sunflower, or lima beans, in each container.

Step 3 ➤ Put one container somewhere warm and sunny; one where it gets a little bit of sun; one in a cupboard.

Step 4 ➤ Water the seeds each day. Record which seeds grow best.

	Warm and sunny	A little bit of sun	In a cupboard
Day 1			
Day 2			
Day 3			

Conclusion What did you learn about the seeds' preferred living conditions from this experiment? Which seeds grew best?